The
LITTLE BOOK OF
GIN

Nick Moyle

summersdale

THE LITTLE BOOK OF GIN

An Hachette UK Company
www.hachette.co.uk

Summersdale Publishers
Part of Octopus Publishing Group Limited
Carmelite House
50 Victoria Embankment
LONDON
EC4Y 0DZ
UK

www.summersdale.com

Printed and bound in China

ISBN: 978-1-83799-397-0

Substantial discounts on bulk quantities of Summersdale books are available to corporations, professional associations and other organizations. For details contact general enquiries: telephone: +44 (0) 1243 771107 or email: enquiries@summersdale.com.

Disclaimer
Neither the author nor the publisher can be held responsible for any injury, loss or claim – be it health, financial or otherwise – arising out of the use, or misuse, of the suggestions made herein. The publisher urges care and caution in the pursuit of any of the activities represented in this book. This book is intended for use by adults only. Please drink responsibly.

Contents

INTRODUCTION
4

GLOSSARY
6

THE WORLD OF GIN
9

TYPES OF GIN
38

FASCINATING FLAVOURS
68

COCKTAIL HOUR
98

HOW WILL YOU DRINK YOURS?
124

Introduction

Gin is a drink that puts a smile on people's faces. It can pick you up after a tough day at the office, it can breathe life into a social occasion and, if you have any excuse for a celebration, gin will gladly join in.

Right now, we are in a golden age for gin. For every well-known classic that has stood the test of time, there are hundreds of new products enticing gin enthusiasts with their vast array of exciting flavours. Style boundaries are being pushed in increasingly new and innovative directions and more countries than ever before are producing gin of exceptional quality.

In this book we'll delve into the history of gin and look at some of the reasons that have made it so successful. We'll help you to navigate the many styles of gin available, learn about the process that goes into making gin and find out more about the botanical ingredients that are used to flavour it. We will show you how to serve gin – from finding its perfect tonic partner to picking the right garnish – and we will teach you how best to appreciate its flavours. And finally, we'll introduce you to some of the best cocktails in which to enjoy it.

There has never been a better time to be a gin fan, so settle down in a comfy chair, pour yourself your favourite type and let's see if we can make that smile even bigger.

Glossary

As you explore the world of gin (and read through this book), you'll come across some technical terms that are used throughout the industry. Here are some of the more common ones you'll encounter:

ABV: Stands for "alcohol by volume", which is a measure of the amount of ethanol (alcohol) in a drink expressed as a percentage.

Cuts: The points during distillation where the distiller separates the fractions. In general practice a first cut will remove the foreshots and heads, and a final cut will remove the tails.

Distillation: The purification of a liquid by converting it into a vapour and condensing it back into a liquid.

Ethanol: The form of alcohol contained in alcoholic drinks.

Fermentation, alcoholic: The process in which sugars are converted into alcohol and carbon dioxide.

Foreshots: The first stuff to come through the still. It's high in methanol (which is poisonous) so is discarded.

Fractions: The various components contained in a mix of compounds that are separated throughout the process of distillation (e.g. foreshots, heads, hearts and tails).

Heads: The compounds (including methanol and acetaldehyde) released after the foreshots during distillation. These are discarded.

Hearts: The distilled spirit produced between the heads and tails that contains the best flavours and is collected for the finished gin.

Low wines: The liquid produced by the first run of distillation – they contain more alcohol than the pre-distilled wash, but less than the final spirit.

Malt: Grains (such as barley) that have been allowed to germinate and dried to convert their starches into sugars and enzymes that are beneficial for fermentation.

Mash: The sugary, watery mix of grains or fruit before it is fermented.

Neutral spirit: A distilled spirit with a highly concentrated ethanol content of above 95 per cent (also called "rectified spirit").

Proof: A measurement for the amount of ethanol (alcohol) in a drink. Historically, the calculation of "proof" has varied, with taxes and the gunpowder "proof test" (see page 51) all used as a gauge. Today, America uses "alcohol proof" as its main measure, with the figure equating to twice the ABV.

Protected Geographical Indication (PGI): A European rule that means a product can only be made in the region whose name it bears.

Rectification: Repeat distillation of alcohol to purify it.

Tails: The last portions of liquid produced by the distillation process. These have lower quantities of ethanol and less desirable flavours so are generally discarded.

Wash: The alcoholic liquid produced by fermentation before it is distilled.

THE WORLD
OF GIN

Gin has become such an established part of contemporary culture that it can be all too easy to take it for granted. Wander into a supermarket or browse the drinks pages of an online retailer and you'll be confronted with a seemingly endless choice of bottles, each boasting its combination of special ingredients, unique production methods or the magical location in which it is made.

But there's a lot more to understanding gin than the latest innovation or flavour craze. Gin has been around for centuries, with precursors existing long before we started to call it gin, and it has been through numerous fluctuations in fortune and fashion over time. So, the next time "gin o'clock" approaches, take a pause before you sip and appreciate that, whatever bottle you've chosen, you'll be delving into a drink with some incredible history.

What is gin?

Gin is a neutral spirit that has been flavoured with juniper and any number of other botanical ingredients. There are several ways in which a gin-maker can obtain the base spirit used as a starting point for their gin, and they can use various methods to tease the flavours and aromas from their chosen botanicals (all of which we will discuss later). But the key ingredient common to all gins is juniper – without it, a spirit flavoured with other botanicals is essentially flavoured vodka.

In the hands of today's artisan gin-makers, the range and quality of gins has never been greater, and the excitement generated by contemporary gins has sparked a worldwide revolution, all of which is good news for the gin enthusiast. But to truly know and appreciate gin, it's important to understand where it comes from and how it's made. So let us start our journey of discovery with that key ingredient, juniper...

A botanical guide to juniper

The most essential flavour of gin comes from the berries of the evergreen juniper, a tree or shrub in the cypress family containing over 60 species. Not all species are edible and, of those that are, it's the common juniper (*Juniperus communis*) that is the most widely used by gin-makers.

Common juniper tends to prefer cooler climates in the northern hemisphere, and it's not especially keen on being cultivated, so harvesting the small purple berries (which are actually the plant's female cones) is often done in the wild by hand.

As with many wild plants, common juniper's natural habitats have been dwindling at an alarming rate, while a disease (*Phytophthora austrocedri*) is further reducing its numbers. The current interest in gin could aid its recovery, with some distilleries restoring juniper populations through ambitious planting projects, but it is a slow grower, taking around twenty years from sowing a seed to harvesting ripe berries – another reason to savour every drop of gin those berries help make.

A history of juniper and alcohol

Gin has a long and interesting history, but the combination of juniper and alcohol goes back much further. Juniper's earliest use was medicinal – Ancient Egyptians used it to treat ailments including headaches and tapeworm. The first evidence of a boozy juniper tonic comes from Greek physician Pedanius Dioscorides who, between 50 CE and 70 CE, wrote a five-volume encyclopaedia about herbal medicines, *De Materia Medica*. In it, he details the use of juniper steeped in wine to combat chest ailments. In 77 CE, naturalist Pliny the Elder advocated juniper in white wine as a cure for stomach ache, cramps and more. Alcohol was used as a way of extracting the medicinal properties from an ingredient, and wine helped offset the bitter flavours.

When it comes to drinking for pleasure there's evidence of juniper being used to flavour a Finnish beer known as *sahti* since the fourteenth century, but it wasn't until distilling became a more refined process that it found its most successful alcoholic match.

A history of juniper and spirits

No one can be certain where or when juniper was first used to flavour a distilled spirit, but many people present a case for Italy. The process of distillation goes back to ancient times (2000 BCE, according to some estimates), although production would have been crude and the aim was usually to make perfumes or medicines.

It wasn't until around 800 CE that distillation became a more refined process, thanks to the introduction of stills, with Arabic alchemist Abu Musa Jabir ibn Hayyan credited as the first to document their use. In the eleventh century, Muslim traders brought stills to Europe where, among others, Benedictine monks at the school of medicine in Salerno, Italy began to use them to make *aqua vitae* (a strong spirit that translates as "water of life"). The monks were already using juniper in wine-based tonics and it seems highly likely that they would have used their stills to produce a spirit flavoured with the same ingredients.

The Dutch introduce genever

As the practice of distillation spread throughout Europe, the Dutch were among the most eager exponents of the art. The Dutch word for juniper, "genever", was eventually adopted as the name for their own juniper-flavoured spirit, which was to greatly influence the drink we now know as gin.

A wine flavoured with juniper was mentioned by Flemish monk Jacob van Maerlant as far back as the 1260s, but the first recording of a distilled beverage using juniper appeared in a book by Antwerp physician Philippus Hermanni, published in 1552. Although early spirits were often distilled from a wine made with grapes, the region was much better suited to growing grains and, from the sixteenth century, spirits were increasingly being distilled from beer (known as "malt wine").

Initially consumed as a medicinal tonic, the Dutch mastery of distillation improved the drink's quality and genever grew in popularity.

Gin in England

In 1689, the English had just disposed of their king, James II, during a period known as the Glorious Revolution. The baton of monarchy was handed down to James's daughter, Mary, who jointly ruled the land with her husband, the Dutchman William III (aka William of Orange). With William came a fashion for genever.

Although English distillers had been producing juniper-flavoured spirits long before William's arrival, the name "genever" caught on and was eventually shortened to "gin" – a much easier word for the English to pronounce, particularly when under the influence of alcohol. While Dutch genevers had more of a grainy flavour as a result of blending malt wine with their juniper-infused spirits, the English tended to prefer their gin without these malty notes and would add flavour to a base spirit, forgoing the additional blending process. These differences are largely what separates the two distinct drinks – gin and genever – today.

THE GIN CRAZE

Following William and Mary's accession to the English throne, laws were passed to encourage distillation of more English gin at the expense of imported French brandy, and its production was opened up to a wider market. Gin had been the fashionable choice among the social elite but, with taxes raised on beer, it quickly became the drink the masses turned to, and they consumed it in great numbers.

Consumption during the first half of the eighteenth century became known as the "gin craze". In 1723, London's death rate exceeded the birth rate, crime was on the rise and Londoners were living in a kind of gin-soaked squalor. While folk were giddy on gin, their babies were being neglected, for which women were held responsible, leading to the phrase "Mother's Ruin".

As vice-chamberlain Lord Hervey noted: "Drunkenness of the common people was universal, the whole town of London swarmed with drunken people from morning till night." Several laws to curb this vice were passed, but with little effect. Something drastic needed to be done.

DID YOU KNOW?

William Hogarth produced his famous 1751 print *Gin Lane* to "reform some reigning Vices peculiar to the lower Class of People", according to the artist. Among the vices depicted are: a baby falling to its death beneath a distracted mother; a boy and dog gnawing on the ends of a bone; a desperate couple pawning possessions to fund their gin habit; and other crazed scenes of death and drunkenness.

Gin is banned!

Gin may not have been responsible for all of London society's ills, but it bore the brunt of the blame. Those in power took a dim view of the poorer classes drowning their sorrows in cheap booze and, rather than looking to improve their lives by other methods, targeted gin. Some of the many measures introduced to curb gin-drinking did indeed reduce consumption, but not enough – by 1749, Londoners had over 17,000 gin shops from which to select their next fix. In 1751, the Tippling Act came into force, increasing both the duty paid on spirits and the cost of a licence to sell it. Six years later, with gin production slowing, a poor harvest prompted lawmakers to ban the distillation of grains altogether. By the time distillation was reintroduced in 1760, beer was the drink of choice and the gin craze was over, but a new phase of gin popularity was about to begin...

Gin goes global

Following the reintroduction of grain-distilling in London, gin began to shrug off its association with the drunken masses. Some of today's biggest brands subsequently came into being, including Greenall's in 1761 and Gordon's in 1769. As distilling quality and efficiency improved, gin started to be more like the product we are familiar with today.

In 1850, gin's export duties were removed and this higher-quality gin started to spread beyond London. It was already becoming popular wherever the British Navy travelled when, in the 1860s, French vineyards were hit by a blight that decimated their crops, and gin was ready to fill the void left by the lack of wine and brandy. In 1870, America could claim its first dry gin distillery, Fleischmann's, and by the end of the century, Beefeater, Seagram's and Tanqueray were all established brands. Producers could also now show off gin's crystal-clear looks thanks to a new breakthrough: clear glass bottles. Gin was going up in the world.

Gin's rise and fall

The early 1900s saw a surge in popularity of cocktails, helped by innovations that made ice more readily available. Desperate to shake off gin's association with loutish behaviour, brands eagerly pushed their products towards the glamorous cocktail market on both sides of the Atlantic. Not even prohibition (1920–1933) could dent gin's popularity. Some of America's most celebrated bartenders headed to Europe to show off their skills, while back home bootleggers would turn to gin botanicals (and cocktails) to hide the crude taste of their spirits.

A period of decline for gin began with the Second World War (1939–1945). Many of Britain's distilleries were destroyed, while those that survived saw grain supplies rationed. In the post-war years, gin's fashionable status diminished. Young folk saw it as a drink associated with their parents' generation and they turned to vodka for their cocktails instead.

Gin's craft revival

If gin was to compete with the clean taste of vodka, not to mention the new flavours found in the rums, liqueurs and aperitifs that were crowding bars, it needed to freshen things up.

As the twentieth century drew to a close, several new gins entered the market that helped to reinvigorate gin's fortunes. In 1986, Bombay Sapphire launched in the UK. This gin pared back the heavy flavours of juniper, proudly showing off all ten of its botanicals and was presented in a daring blue glass bottle.

In 1999, Hendrick's began making a gin that infused rose and cucumber into a blend of spirits, sending flavour possibilities in new directions. By now, Australia was also producing gin, following the launch of the Lark Distillery in 1992, and gin's world domination was under way.

If Bombay Sapphire paved the way for gins that were less reliant on juniper as a flavour, in 2006, Aviation American Gin reduced its use to a minimum, creating a style known as New Western Dry, which allowed other botanicals an equal share of the limelight.

Back in the UK, an old law that stipulated a minimum size for pot stills was removed in 2009, allowing Sipsmith's distillery and Chase Distillery to take advantage by producing small-batch craft spirits. The following year, a law that prevented breweries from distilling was lifted, further opening up the market. Gin's revival was in full swing and the world's taste for it grew at an astonishing pace.

The gin boom shows no signs of slowing. Gin drinkers can enjoy products from all corners of the globe, drink at any number of dedicated gin bars and festivals, and join gin clubs, tasting events and guided tours of distilleries. And with new flavours constantly being dreamt up, the world of gin continues to evolve at a rapid rate.

Gin meets tonic

Gin might not have become the all-conquering spirit superstar it is today if it hadn't been acquainted with tonic water. It's difficult to think of two other drinks that have formed more of a successful partnership.

The two first met in India during the mid-nineteenth century. As with early juniper drinks, tonic was originally used as a medicine. Its main ingredient, quinine, which is extracted from the bark of South American cinchona trees, was the best thing known for treating – and preventing – malaria. Quinine was used by the British Army stationed in India, but its bitterness was a little too unpleasant for sensitive palates. To improve its flavour, the Army began mixing it with soda water and sugar, thus creating what became known as "Indian Tonic Water". Before long, tonic water was being mixed with gin and marketed as a cocktail, no longer seen simply as a cure for malaria. Today's tonics come in a variety of flavours, but it's still the bitter quinine that brings out the best in gin.

The gin and tonic has saved more Englishmen's lives, and minds, than all the doctors in the Empire.

Winston Churchill

Making gin: an overview

Now we know that gin is a neutral spirit flavoured with juniper and other botanicals, so it follows that anyone who wants to make gin first needs to get their hands on a spirit. Although some distilleries make their own spirits on site, it involves extra equipment, time and effort, so the vast majority buy their base spirits from elsewhere.

The process of making the base spirit begins with creating alcohol through the fermentation of a sugary liquid. This low-alcohol liquid is then distilled to concentrate the alcohol into a clear, colourless form. There are various ways in which flavour can be added to this high-strength spirit but the most common is through redistilling it with the botanicals, extracting the oils and compounds that contain the all-important aromas and flavours. We will take a closer look at these stages later, but first we need to rewind to that sugary liquid and find out what ingredients it comes from...

The raw ingredients for spirit-making

Most spirits must be made from specified ingredients in order to meet their industry's requirements, but gin and vodka can be made using anything. Here are the ingredients most commonly used, with each one lending subtly differing tastes and textures to the finished gin.

GRAINS

Grains are the most used ingredients for making the base spirits destined for gins, with wheat and barley topping the list. Other grains used include rye, oats and corn. Head to Uganda and you might be offered *waragi*, a type of gin made from millet.

RICE

In Japan, rice is commonly used to make a base spirit. You might also come across gins that use *shōchū* as their base – a traditional Japanese spirit distilled from a number of grains, vegetables and sugar.

FRUIT

Grapes have a strong historical association with gin production, while you might also see the occasional bottle that has been initially distilled from apples.

SUGAR

Rum is the best-known drink distilled from sugar and it's a base spirit that also makes good gin. Most commonly molasses is used – a dark syrup made by processing sugar cane – but it can also be made from fresh cane juice.

POTATOES

More commonly associated with vodka, potato-based spirits are being increasingly used by gin-makers, giving the spirit a slightly creamy texture.

WHEY

This is a by-product of dairy production that contains lactose, which can be fermented into alcohol. As it's a product that would otherwise be discarded, its sustainable appeal could mean we will see more whey-based gins in future (although these aren't suitable for vegans).

Extracting sugar

Before creating alcohol, sugars must be extracted from the raw ingredients. For most fruits and sugar cane, this is simply done by crushing or pressing them to release juice, while other ingredients, such as potatoes and beet, are heated to release the sugar.

For most grains, the process is a little more complicated, as they contain starches that first need to be converted into sugar. Some grains can be ground and have enzymes added to them, which convert starches to sugar, while others, notably barley, go through a process known as "malting".

This involves steeping the grains in water until they germinate, before drying and milling. The malted grains are then added to water and heated to a specific temperature (known as "mashing") to extract the starch, with natural enzymes converting it into sugar. Malted barley is often added to other grains as its enzymes will also act on their starches.

The sugary liquid, known as a "wort", is added to a fermenter, where the magic really begins to happen...

Fermentation

Fermentation is the process of converting sugars into something different by the use of microorganisms. In the case of alcohol, yeast is the microorganism that performs this special trick on sugar.

Yeast is all around us and particularly likes nestling on fruits. This means that it is entirely possible to create alcohol by simply crushing fruits and leaving them in a suitable fermentation vessel (many ciders and wines are made this way), while other sugary liquids can be exposed to the air to attract wild yeasts that start the fermentation process.

However, wild yeasts can be a little unpredictable so, for spirit-making, commercial yeasts are more often used, to offer a bit more control. Yeast is added to the liquid where it feeds on the sugar, converting it to alcohol and carbon dioxide. Depending on the ingredients used and fermentation conditions, this can take a matter of hours or several weeks. When complete, the liquid – now known as the "wash" – is ready to be distilled.

Distillation to produce a spirit base

Distillation is a process by which a liquid is boiled and condensed in order to separate its components. In spirit-making, this means heating the wash to separate the ethanol (the alcohol we want to drink) from the water (and other unwanted stuff).

There are two main types of still that can be used to perform this task - a pot still and a column still, which we will look at more closely on pages 35–36. Generally, column stills are most commonly used to create the highly concentrated base spirit, while pot stills are used to extract flavour and aromas from the botanicals used to make gin.

To understand how the process of distilling alcohol works, we should note that ethanol has a lower boiling point (78°C) than water (100°C). By heating the wash in a still, the ethanol contained within the liquid will start to vaporize before the water. These vapours rise up through the still where they are collected and condensed (cooled) back into liquid form.

By carefully managing the process of heating, collecting and cooling, the distiller is not only able to leave the water behind, but it can also strip out any impurities, reducing the alcohol to a purer spirit. First to be removed are volatile compounds known as "foreshots" and "heads". Next comes the good stuff to be collected, which is referred to as the "hearts" or "spirit". Towards the end of distillation, compounds with less desirable flavours (known as the "tails" or "faints") will come through so the distiller will "cut" the process to retain only the hearts.

The distillation process can be repeated (known as "rectification") to increase the alcohol's strength and purity.

Depending on the raw ingredients used, and the strength achieved, this alcohol can be put into barrels to become whisky, bourbon, brandy or other aged spirits, or it can be diluted, bottled and sold as familiar drinks that include white rum and vodka. For use as a base in gin, a minimum strength of 96 per cent ABV is the aim.

Distillation to add flavour and aroma

Besides reaching boiling point before water, alcohol also has another skill that is invaluable to drinks makers – it acts as a solvent that can extract the essential oils from botanicals that are responsible for flavour and aroma.

While ingredients can simply be infused in alcohol to extract their flavours, for most gins, an additional stage of distillation is used.

The base spirit has its strength reduced with water and is then redistilled with the gin-maker's chosen botanicals. Traditionally, these would be steeped in the spirit before the liquid is put back through the distillation process, but other methods are also used. "Vapour infusion" sees the ingredients placed in baskets above the spirit so its vapour extracts the flavour, while "vacuum distillation" involves redistilling under a vacuum to reduce the temperature at which the ethanol boils.

We will see how these varying processes can affect flavour in the next chapter.

DID YOU KNOW?

The heads and tails removed from the spirit during distillation don't always go to waste. As these cuts still contain some ethanol, distillers often add them to the next batch of liquid to run through the still. Alternatively, they can be recycled to make hand sanitizer, a practice that rapidly increased as a result of the Covid-19 pandemic.

Stills

THE POT STILL

The still that is most commonly associated with gin production is the pot still, generally used to extract the flavours from botanical ingredients. As you might guess, it is like a giant pot that heats the alcoholic liquid you wish to distil.

When the alcohol boils, its vapours rise to the top of the pot and are drawn into a narrow tube before making their way through a condenser. This condenser is cooled with running water, turning the vapour back into liquid that can be collected, now with a much higher ethanol content. Once this batch is completed, the still is emptied and cleaned ready for the next batch.

> The forerunner to the modern pot still was the "alembic still". Copper is the preferred material for pot stills and they are often referred to as simply "copper pots".

THE COLUMN STILL

This is a much more efficient still that is commonly used to create base spirits. Also known as a "continuous still", the distiller can continuously add fermented liquid (the wash) to the top of a column. The column contains a series of plates, creating chambers that operate a bit like mini pot stills.

Steam is sent into the bottom of the column and rises, meeting the falling wash. This steam turns the wash into vapour, which condenses every time it hits a plate. The lighter alcohol vapours continue to rise, while the heavier wash falls back down through the column. The rising alcohol vapours become more concentrated every time they pass through a plate before being diverted, condensed and collected as high-strength alcohol. For even purer alcohol, columns can be linked together.

The "Coffey still" is an early type of column still patented by Irishman Aeneas Coffey in 1830 that vastly improved distilling quality and efficiency. It's also known as a "patent still".

*My main ambition
as a gardener is to
water my orange trees
with gin. Then all I
have to do is squeeze
the juice into
a glass.*

W. C. Fields

TYPES OF GIN

Gin comes in many guises. A juniper-heavy London Dry gin (page 42) can seem a world away from a blackcurrant- and ginger-flavoured gin, yet they are both gins. Understanding what the different styles of gin mean not only helps you find where your preferences lie but can also be useful in determining what bottle to buy when making cocktails.

And as if there weren't enough gin styles to get to grips with, some gins are also defined by the various flavouring techniques used to create them. Translating all of those terms into a simple understanding of what the gin might actually taste like can, at times, seem a challenging proposition.

In this chapter, we'll look at the main gin styles, along with some of those other terms you might encounter. But first let's check in on the key legal definitions of just what can be called "gin".

The legal definitions of gin

Although not as strictly defined as other spirits such as whisky, tequila or brandy, there are boundaries as to what can be labelled "gin", with the degree of flexibility gin-makers are afforded depending on where they are in the world. Here are some of the main laws governing the industry:

THE EU AND UK

According to EU and UK law, gin must be made from ethyl alcohol and predominantly flavoured with juniper. There is no definition as to what "predominant" might mean, but it has to come from the common juniper (*Juniperus communis*). Gin-makers are also permitted to use approved artificial flavours, as well as natural ingredients, which could include alternative varieties of juniper along with a whole host of other botanicals. Gin can also be sweetened or have colouring added and can be diluted with water to a minimum bottling strength of 37.5 per cent ABV.

THE US

The US Gin Association defines gin as "a neutral grain spirit redistilled with the addition of juniper, typically with the addition of other botanicals and aromatics". It must be bottled at a minimum of 80 proof (the equivalent of 40 per cent ABV) and have "a main characteristic flavour derived from juniper berries produced by distillation or mixing of spirits with juniper berries and other aromatics or extracts". Any variety of juniper can be used.

AUSTRALIA AND NEW ZEALAND

The only legal definitions for gin in Australia and New Zealand are those that relate to spirits in general, namely "a potable alcoholic distillate, including whisky, rum, gin, vodka and tequila", which contains "at least 37 per cent ABV, produced by distillation of fermented liquor derived from food sources". Although each spirit must have "the taste, aroma and other characteristics generally attributable to that particular spirit", this technically means that gin doesn't even need to contain juniper. However, producers will generally follow American and European conventions.

Distilled gin

Although all gin starts off with a distilled spirit, if you see a bottle that has "distilled gin" on the label, it means that the neutral alcohol used as a base has been through a process of redistillation in a traditional still, along with the chosen botanicals. "Distilled gin" is defined in law by the EU and the UK, with enough leeway to allow additional flavourings, sweeteners and colourings to be added to the gin after it has been redistilled.

London gin

This style follows the definitions of distilled gin but with a key difference: once it has been redistilled with the chosen botanicals, nothing else may be added except water, to bring it down to bottle strength. Although this method of gin production originated in London, gins made anywhere in the world can be labelled "London gin".

This style is adopted by most of the successful, established gin brands, including Gordon's, Greenall's and Beefeater.

Quite often you'll see London gins labelled "London Dry gin". The term "dry" relates to the fact that, without the post-distillation addition of sweeteners or sweet ingredients, the gin maintains a crisp, dry bite to it.

Producers will often label such dry gins by switching "London" for their own location, an example being gin from The Botanist, labelled "Islay Dry Gin" after its Scottish island home. This gin is flavoured by steeping and distilling nine base botanicals, with more flavours and aromas teased out by vapour extraction from another 22 botanicals collected on Islay.

Tanqueray London Dry is a great example of the style and uses just four botanicals – juniper, coriander seeds, angelica and liquorice root.

Although contemporary gin-makers summon a whole host of botanicals to create complexity in their London gins, the best ones complement the juniper without allowing any of the other ingredients to dominate.

Vapour-infused gin

The traditional method of extracting flavours and aromas from botanicals involves immersing them in the base spirit before distilling. With vapour extraction, the botanicals never come into contact with the liquid spirit.

Instead, they are placed in a basket that is held inside the still above the spirit. When the spirit is heated, its vapours rise and pass through the basket of botanicals, taking with them their congeners (aroma compounds), which remain locked within the gin when it is condensed back into a liquid.

As the temperature of the vapour that passes through the botanicals is lower than the hot liquid below, it only picks up the lighter compounds, leading to more delicately flavoured gins. The method suits botanicals that may not withstand being submerged in hot liquid, such as fresh flowers or citrus fruits, and distillers can also change the botanicals in the basket at any stage, giving them more control. Bombay Sapphire uses vapour infusion for its game-changing, lighter style of gin.

DID YOU KNOW?

Greenall's, founded in 1761 by Thomas Dakin,
lays claim to being the oldest gin distillery
in England. In 2023, the distillery showed
a vision for the future of gin by releasing
its London Dry gin in a bottle made from a
mostly paper-based material. This lighter,
more easily recyclable packaging has a carbon
footprint six times lower than a glass bottle.

Vacuum-distilled gin

When botanicals are subjected to heat, they are, to some degree, cooked. While this cooking of ingredients has little effect on the flavours and aromas extracted from some botanicals, for others it can drastically alter them. Vacuum distillation, also known as "cold distillation", is a way of extracting flavours from botanicals without the need for heat, allowing distillers to work with much more delicate ingredients.

Rather than heat, the pressure inside the still is reduced to create a vacuum, enabling the ethanol to evaporate at a much lower temperature. The higher the vacuum, the lower the temperature at which distillation can take place. This also allows different flavours to come to the fore than would through traditional distillation.

Oxley Cold Distilled London Dry gin is a good example of how this technique works, with the distillers using fresh, frozen citrus peel (instead of the usual dried peels) among 14 botanicals that are distilled at -5°C. This gives a fresh, zesty lift to the aroma of the finished gin.

Multi-shot distillation

As we have learned, the traditional method of making gin involves distilling all of the botanicals together, with the resulting spirit being diluted with water to bring it to the desired strength for bottling. The distiller ends up with a single batch of bottles from each distillation (this is known as "single-shot" distillation).

With "multi-shot distillation", enough botanicals are added to the still for several batches of bottles, producing a spirit with a greater concentration of aroma and flavour. This concentrate is then diluted with base spirit to bring the botanical flavours to the desired level (i.e. comparable to a single-shot distillation) before the water is added for bottling.

In theory, this method should have little or no impact on the overall quality of the gin (although some craft single-shotters may disagree), but it does have an impact on efficiency. More bottles can be produced from each distillation, saving the distiller on energy costs which, in turn, is beneficial for the environment.

Cold compounded gins

A cold compounded gin is one that has been flavoured by infusing botanical ingredients (or botanical essences) into a base spirit, rather than extracting their flavours and aromas through distillation. Some see this as an inferior process – it was once used as a crude way of masking the flavour of poor-quality spirits and, if not done carefully, can result in less desirable compounds dissolving in the alcohol, producing unwanted flavours and aromas. The process also adds colour to the gin.

However, many fruits are particularly suited to this method and some contemporary gin-makers use the technique to enrich spirits with fruity flavours. Tappers makes various compounded gins, including its seasonal Figgy Pudding Christmas Gin, which is made by infusing juniper, figs and other ingredients in neutral spirit to create a gin full of festive pudding flavours.

You may also come across the term "bathtub gin", an old name for compounded gins, deriving from the vessel sometimes used to carry out the task.

MAKE YOUR OWN COLD COMPOUNDED GIN

Seeing as no distilling equipment is needed to make a cold compounded gin, it's something anyone can do in their own home. If you want to have a go yourself then you'll need to start with a neutral spirit, so grab a bottle of vodka. Then simply add your chosen botanicals to the vodka and wait for it to take on your desired gin flavours.

As the key ingredient to gin is juniper berries, it's essential these are among them – try a tablespoon or two per 70-cl bottle of vodka, depending on how juniper-heavy you want it. Add just a pinch or two of your chosen botanicals – a few coriander seeds and some dried lemon or orange peel make a great start, but see the ingredients section from page 71 for more inspiration.

Allow it to infuse overnight before testing the flavour – you can either leave it for longer or add more ingredients if desired – and straining and bottling.

Plymouth gin

While folk in London were enjoying the intoxicating properties of the vast amounts of gin available to them during the gin craze, another city, Plymouth, on England's south coast, was also doing a roaring trade in the spirit. Plymouth's distilleries were supplying its gin to the Royal Navy and, unlike much of the crude booze produced in the capital, the quality was said to be consistently high.

For a while, Plymouth gin had a Protected Geographical Indication (PGI), meaning it could only be produced in Plymouth, but this status lapsed in 2014 and so it can technically be made anywhere.

Now the city has only one distillery, the Plymouth Distillery (also known as Black Friars), and its Plymouth gin, produced there since 1793, is a little softer, deeper and earthier than the archetypical London Dry. It makes a great G&T, works well in most cocktails and, for style and taste, really is one of a kind.

Navy-strength gin

If gin (or rum) is bottled at a strength of 57.15 per cent ABV or higher, then it can be deemed to be "navy strength". The term comes from when Royal Navy vessels stored gunpowder and booze below deck.

While there are many reasons alcohol and gunpowder shouldn't mix, the Navy's concern was the risk of spirit spilling into the gunpowder and rendering it useless. However, strong alcohol is flammable, so the gunpowder could still be successfully ignited if it came into contact with spirits of sufficient strength. It was therefore important that any barrels kept on ship contained alcohol strong enough to be flammable. A "proof test" was required for spirits to be allowed on board, with those passing being certified "100 degrees proof" (or "gunpowder proof").

The Isle of Wight Distillery, in a region with strong naval associations, produces HMS Victory Gin, which passes the proof test. As is usually the case with navy-strength gins, the strong alcohol is matched by bold flavours, with juniper, pepper and citrus all to the fore.

Old Tom gin

For a period in the eighteenth and nineteenth centuries, Old Tom was an incredibly popular style of gin. It was slightly sweetened, likely coming about as a way of masking poor-quality spirits, but even as distillation methods improved, a desire for this sweet style remained, particularly among cocktail makers, who often used Old Toms when conjuring new recipes.

As the unsweetened London Dry style became more popular towards the end of the nineteenth century, Old Tom gins fell out of fashion and it's only in recent times the style has undergone a revival. During its heyday, sweetening wasn't always done with sugar, with liquorice being commonly used in its place – its strong flavour also helped to mask inferior spirits. Today, distillers are exploring a variety of sweeteners, such as honey, for their Old Toms, and digging up old recipes that relied on liquorice and other botanicals for sweetness.

Old Toms work in any classic gin cocktail including a Martini (page 102) and a Tom Collins (page 114).

I've tried Buddhism, Scientology, Numerology, Transcendental Meditation, Qabbala, t'ai chi, feng shui and Deepak Chopra but I find straight gin works best.

Phyllis Diller

New Western Dry gin

This is a term used to describe gins that are less reliant on juniper as a dominant flavour. Bombay Sapphire and Hendrick's were early adopters of this approach, but it was Ryan Magarian, one of the co-founders of Aviation American Gin, who came up with the term.

Although juniper is still very much an essential ingredient, some New Western Dry gins do push the boundaries on whether it remains the predominant flavour. The best examples tend to have juniper working in harmony with the other distinctive flavours.

Despite sounding like a regional classification, that wasn't the intention, and these gins are made the world over, although some distilleries prefer to use more generic terms like "contemporary gin" or "new age gin" instead.

You will also find similar contemporary gins grouped by their region of production, with ingredients common to their location prominent among the flavours. A good example are Mediterranean gins, with their focus on local floral, herbal and citrus flavours.

Gin de Mahón

Menorca is a tiny Balearic island in the Mediterranean, with a population of under 100,000. Its capital, Mahón, has one distillery, Destilerías Xoriguer, but there was a time when it had several more, a result of it being under British rule during most of the eighteenth century.

And yet, despite being a one-distillery city, the gin it produces has a rare EU PGI and rules that govern how its Gin de Mahón is made. Perhaps the most unusual aspect of these rules are the botanicals permitted: common juniper, and nothing else. The alcohol must be between 38 per cent and 43 per cent and distilled in copper stills over a wood fire.

When drinking this gin, you are simply tasting the base spirit and the juniper, with all its zesty, resinous pine flavours. To enjoy it at its best, drink it like the locals, chilled in the fridge and served neat. Or mix up the island's own party cocktail, the Pomada – three parts lemonade, one part gin and a wedge of lemon.

Genever

As we have learned, genever had a huge influence on the development of gin in the eighteenth century, but gin and genever aren't the same thing. Genever is actually a blend of two different liquids – malt wine and juniper-infused neutral spirit. While neutral spirit is the high-strength alcohol used as a base for gins, malt wine is distilled from a mix of grains to lower strength (around 50 per cent) and so it contains more grainy flavours, along with a few impurities. True genevers can only be produced in its historical heartlands of the Netherlands, Belgium, two regions in France (Pas-de-Calais and Nord) and two states in Germany (Lower Saxony and North Rhine-Westphalia).

Genever or jenever?

Confusingly, "genever" has a few alternative names and spellings, including "jenever", "Geneva" and even "hollands".

DIFFERENT STYLES OF GENEVER

There are various styles of genever available, with the main ones being as follows:

Oude genever: Although it means "old genever", this has nothing to do with the age of the drink, but rather the fact that it is made with traditional (i.e. older) techniques. It must be a minimum strength of 35 per cent ABV and contain at least 15 per cent malt wine. It often has a golden hue from the addition of caramel.

Jonge genever: "Young" genevers are made by more modern distilling processes, must be at least 35 per cent ABV and contain a maximum of 15 per cent malt wine.

Graanjenever: "Grain" genevers must be distilled only from grains.

Korenwijn: Made with at least 51 per cent malt wine, this doesn't have to contain juniper (it is technically not a true genever).

Besides these main classifications, you can also find aged and flavoured genevers. To try the full range of styles, look out for genevers produced by Lucas Bols, the oldest distillery brand in the world.

Flavoured gin

This is a term used to describe a gin that promotes one or two botanicals as a standout flavour. There are no laws governing what might constitute a flavoured gin, and the star ingredient can be added before, during or after distillation – either fresh or in the form of artificial flavourings. With some of these gins, the promoted ingredient works alongside the juniper, while in others it might come dangerously close to relegating juniper to an "also-ran" botanical.

Although fruits are the most common ingredients for such gins, nothing is off-limits, and you'll find bottles shouting flavours as varied as blackberries, quince, elderflower and marmalade.

Four Pillars Bloody Shiraz is a leader in the category, made by steeping shiraz grapes in distilled gin for maximum flavour, producing the distillery's alternative to sloe gin.

Besides adding a favourite flavour to your next G&T, these gins can also help to extend the cocktail-maker's repertoire when used as a substitute for other flavoured liqueurs and spirits.

DID YOU KNOW?

Some gins turn cloudy when diluted with water, an effect known as "louching". This happens when essential oils that have been totally dissolved in the spirit come out when the ethanol content is lowered, scattering the light to make the liquid appear milky. Some distillers remove the oils through a process known as "chill filtration", while others leave them in, arguing that cloudiness is a small price to pay for their extra flavour.

Barrel-aged gin

As with other spirits, some gins are aged in barrels to impart new flavours into the spirit and modify those that already exist. Sometimes these barrels will have been charred first, coating them in charcoal that acts as a filter to remove some harsher flavours and mellowing the drink.

Besides the wood infusing its flavours into the spirit, the barrels might have previously been used to age another drink such as sherry, rum or bourbon, and their residual flavours will also be present in the finished gin. The longer a spirit is rested in a barrel, the darker it becomes and the more its flavour changes, with air contact and evaporation also having an effect.

When Old Toms were the gin of choice in the eighteenth century, many of them would have been barrel-aged. Boatyard Distillery's Old Tom echoes the process with a gin that has spent time in Pedro Ximénez sherry casks, donating its sweet fruit flavours to the spirit. Sip neat or serve as a whisky replacement in an Old Fashioned.

Gin liqueurs

If definitions surrounding gin styles can seem a little vague at times, then ready yourself for even more potential confusion as we take a look at liqueurs.

A liqueur is essentially a spirit that has been flavoured and sweetened. EU law doesn't distinguish gin liqueurs from other liqueurs, which must contain a minimum of 15 per cent ABV and 100 g sugar per litre. However, in the US, a gin liqueur (where it may also be called "gin cordial") does have its own definition; it must be a minimum of 30 per cent ABV and is supposed to have the predominant flavour of gin.

So, although these drinks can have the word "gin" printed on the bottles, they are not technically gins (too sweet and not enough alcohol or juniper flavouring). Just like flavoured gins, you'll find these liqueurs showing off all sorts of flavours, but there's one gin-based liqueur that stands out all on its own. Turn the page and acquaint yourself with sloe gin...

Sloe gin

Sloes, the small, round, purple fruits of the blackthorn, aren't afforded many culinary opportunities to flaunt their flavours, but give them a bottle of gin and they'll show just what they can do. The sour fruit notes coming from the flesh and mellow almond from the stones make sloe gin the most well-known gin-based liqueur.

Although a British liqueur institution, it's in the US that you'll find laws governing its style, which include a minimum 2.5 per cent sugar by weight and a flavour focus on the sloes (relegating juniper down the order).

There are hundreds of sloe gins on the market, from sickly, syrupy affairs to those that mostly rely on the sloes themselves for sweetness. A good example comes from Sipsmith, where the sloes impart rich, plummy, sweet and sour fruit flavours to their London Dry gin.

Great sipped neat for a bit of winter warmth and comfort, sloe gin can also be added to a cocktail such as a Sloe Negroni (page 110).

HOW TO MAKE SLOE GIN

Tradition has it that the blackthorn bush's thorns would be used to prick sloes' skins prior to soaking them in gin, while another tradition dictates that the sloes should be picked after the first frost of winter to be at their best. But anyone interested in making their own sloe gin can do away with tradition.

To make your own, gather around 450 g of sloes and break their skins with something more practical than a thorn, like a knife or fork (and if you want to beat the frosts, put them in the freezer first) then place in a lidded jar containing 70 cl of gin (a standard London Dry gin will suffice). You can add the sugar at this stage (approximately 220 g is a decent amount), giving it an occasional shake to help it dissolve, or sweeten to taste when ready. A good sloe gin can't be rushed, so wait for at least two months – much longer if you can – before straining and bottling.

Low-alcohol substitutes

For those who want to enjoy the flavours of gin but without the alcohol, there's an increasing number of low- and no-alcohol alternatives available. These tend to be made by distilling gin as normal, but with a vastly greater ratio of botanicals to spirit than usual, resulting in a gin that has a much higher concentration of flavours.

This gin is then diluted down to the requisite strength – often around 0.5 per cent ABV for a negligible amount of alcohol or between 10 per cent ABV and 20 per cent ABV for gins that are lighter on the alcohol. You can also find gins at 0.0 per cent ABV, which have the alcohol entirely removed from them, usually by further processes of distillation. Without the legal amount of alcohol needed to be labelled "gin", these drinks have to come up with other names. Some cunning examples are Lyre's Dry London Spirit and Warner's Botanic GDN Spirits, while more familiar gin brands, such as Tanqueray, are happy to simply display "alcohol free 0.0" beneath their logo.

A man must defend his home, his wife, his children, and his Martini.

Jackie Gleason

Other types of gin

You've now learned the main types of gin available, but there are many more categories and subcategories that you might come across. Here are a few of them:

CONTINENTAL METHOD

In this method, named for being more popular on continental Europe rather than in the UK, all of the botanicals are distilled individually, or in groups, with the separate spirits blended together to produce the finished gin (they are often referred to as "blended gins").

VILNIUS GIN

Besides Gin de Mahón there is one other gin that has geographical protection: Vilnius gin, named after the capital of Lithuania. Among the ingredients and specifications Vilnius distillers must adopt are using local Lithuanian rye, wheat and triticale (a rye and wheat hybrid), juniper (of course), sweet orange and local water with a specific hardness.

PINK GIN

There's a nineteenth-century cocktail known as a "pink gin" (consisting of gin with a dash of Angostura) but more recently the term has been used to describe a category of gins that have a pink blush to them. This colouration is achieved by infusing red ingredients into the gin after distillation, with strawberry, raspberry and rhubarb among the most commonly used.

COASTAL GIN

As with most styles, there are no rules attached to what can be labelled a coastal gin but, besides coastal herbs and flowers, expect the botanical roll call to include such items as seaweeds, samphire, sea buckthorn and even the occasional pinch of sea salt.

ORGANIC GIN

To be labelled "organic", all of the ingredients that go into a gin need to be certified as organic, from those that make the base spirit to the botanicals used to flavour the gin. This can prove to be quite a challenge, hence there's a very limited number of organic gins available.

FASCINATING
FLAVOURS

You now know the history of gin, how it's made, and the different styles of gin available. But what do they really taste like? As we have discovered, gin can cover a huge variety of aromas and flavours, with an infinite choice of botanical combinations available to the gin-maker. When it comes to figuring out which ones you're likely to enjoy, picking a bottle can sometimes seem like a bit of a gamble.

In this chapter we're going to delve into some of the more common flavour profiles you will find on the shelves (along with a few of the wilder options out there) and discover what you can expect when you taste them, along with the best ways to appreciate their unique characteristics.

But first we'll look at some of the key botanicals in a little more detail and the flavours and aromas they'll lend to those gins.

Juniper

We introduced you to gin's star ingredient on page 12, but what kind of flavour does this brilliant botanical actually provide? Bite into one and you may well spit it out in an instant, but immerse some in alcohol and their complex array of flavours become much more appealing. You should detect some wood and resinous pine with a hint of bitterness; perhaps you'll also notice some slightly sweet and sour citrus and berry fruitiness; and there will be some warming, aromatic pepper notes too.

With so much complexity in one ingredient it's little wonder that juniper works so well with just about any other flavour. Next, we will meet some of its main gin companions...

Core botanicals

There is no clear consensus on what you might term a "core botanical", but most gins will have at least a few of these ingredients:

CORIANDER SEEDS

If juniper could name its second in command, then it would likely choose coriander seeds. Coming from the same herb whose leaves are scattered on curries, the round seeds may be small, but they contain a big burst of flavours. There are subtly dry, dusty, spicy notes that help other flavours to shine, and hits of citrus that punctuate those gins that use it. Distillers mostly source coriander seeds from Morocco or Eastern Europe, with flavour varying in character depending on where they come from.

ANGELICA ROOT

Think of gin as an orchestra. There are lots of instruments that hit the high notes (fruits, flowers and some spices)

but to be well-rounded, you also need instruments to provide the low notes. This is where angelica root comes in, with its earthy, woody character chugging along in the background helping to hold gin's more exciting flavours together.

ORRIS ROOT

Orris root comes from two varieties of iris and is used by distillers less for its flavour and more for its ability as a binding agent. It's used in the perfume industry for these same skills, fixing aromas so that subtler scents aren't lost. Happily for the gin-maker, it also comes with a pleasant perfume of its own that is not too dissimilar to violet. It also has a few earthy flavours that act as a companion to angelica.

LIQUORICE ROOT

This may be another root that has some earthy notes to it, but besides its distinctive aniseed-like flavour, liquorice offers many more qualities for the gin distiller. Key among these is a natural sweetness, which is of particular value to Old Tom gins. Liquorice root can also help to enhance the feel of the liquid, giving it a softer, more rounded texture in the mouth.

LEMON PEEL

It's obvious what characteristics lemons can deliver to a bottle of gin: bright, fresh, juicy citrus. For distillers, it's the peel of the lemon that is commonly used as that's where the most flavoursome oils are more concentrated. There are many different varieties of lemon around the world and distillers will increasingly name these varieties to mark their gin out as being different – look out for Fino, Amalfi and Sorrento lemons, among others, and see if you can taste what makes each one stand out.

ORANGE PEEL

Although offering some of the juicy, citrus qualities of lemons, oranges can also provide different levels of bitterness or sweetness depending on the varieties used. As with lemons, oranges tend to be peeled by hand as soon as they're picked and immediately set out to dry, mostly under a hot Spanish sun where those destined for gin are commonly grown.

CASSIA BARK

Cassia is a relative of cinnamon and both are used by the gin-maker for those familiar sweet and warming spicy aromas and flavours that make them such a hit at Christmas. Cassia tends to deliver a bit more heat to a gin than cinnamon and is a touch sweeter too. Both are sold dried, rolled into sticks and, confusingly, cassia bark will often be labelled as cinnamon.

CARDAMOM

Cardamom is prized for its tiny aromatic black seeds, which are deceptively potent, so gin-makers use them in small doses. The complexity of aromas and flavours obtained from cardamom is unlike anything else, so you'll hear all sorts of comparisons when reading tasting notes – from sweet citrus and gingery spice, to floral, herbal and menthol notes. The seeds come in pods, which are either black or green depending on variety, and it's the more subtle, green-podded seeds that tend to get the nod from distillers.

DID YOU KNOW?

Juniper trees grow very slowly and can live to be very old. The largest in America, the Bennett Juniper in Tuolumne County, California, is 24 m high and is a contender for the oldest tree in the world. Part of its trunk is hollow, meaning a definitive age cannot be calculated, but estimations place it anywhere between 2,000 and 6,000 years old.

Spicy botanicals

Besides those among the core botanicals, here are a few of the many more spices used by distillers:

Grains of paradise: A complex spice that goes extremely well with juniper, adding to its bitter, woody and peppery flavours.

Ginger: This root can quickly bring on the heat but, when used sparingly, helps lend a clean, invigorating quality to a gin.

Aniseed: The distinctive earthy notes of aniseed come in several spices that include star anise, fennel, anise and caraway.

Bay leaf: A bit herbal and a bit spicy, this aromatic leaf is a great all-rounder.

Vanilla: A sweeter spice, some vanillas can also bring a hint of smoke and aged wood to a gin.

Black peppercorns: Along with the similar cubeb, these provide various degrees of heat and flavour.

Pink peppercorns: A milder pepper used more for its fruity flavours than its heat.

Fruity botanicals

Fruits destined for the gin distillery generally fall into one of two broad camps: citrus fruits, which add their fresh, zesty vibrancy to gins; and berries, which often get headline status in flavoured gins. Look out for these fruity favourites:

Citrus fruits: Besides lemons and oranges, you'll also often encounter grapefruit and lime, displaying their own twist on the citrus theme, and the sour yuzu, with its grapefruit and orange flavours and strong, zesty aroma.

Berries: Some berries, such as raspberries, are used in small doses within an array of botanicals for their tart, fruity characteristics, but they are more usually deployed as the headline act in flavoured gins. Other popular flavours include strawberry, blackberry, blueberry and cherry.

Orchard fruits: Apples, pears and quince are all popular choices for flavoured gins and liqueurs.

Other fruits commonly used for flavoured gins include plums, peaches and, of course, sloes, which you can read more about on page 62.

Floral botanicals

Distillers need to use flowers with care. Some delicate floral aromas can quickly be lost, while more pungent perfumes, like lavender, can easily overpower other aromas and flavours within the gin. Here are some of the most widely used floral botanicals:

Elderflower: Highly fragrant, it gives a summery freshness to gins.

Camomile: Has subtle fruity notes along with hints of dried grass.

Lavender: A unique taste that combines its calming perfumes with slightly tingly, herby flavours.

Jasmine: A delicate floral aroma and flavour that is faintly sweet.

Hibiscus: Has tart berry flavours with warmer, earthier notes.

Other popular floral botanicals include the uniquely heady perfumes of rose and honeysuckle, the summer hay fragrance of meadowsweet and, for a Japanese influence, the delicate fruity flavours of sakura (cherry) blossom.

Herbal and leafy botanicals

Herbs are largely used in gin as they are in the kitchen
– to bring out and complement the flavours of other
ingredients, adding layers of interest to the overall drink.
Gin-friendly herbs and leaves include the following:

Basil: A sweet herb with savoury notes of anise and mint.

Rosemary: The complex flavours of rosemary can
provide hints of citrus, pine, tingly mint, and a slightly
astringent bitterness.

Tea leaves: Black tea, green tea, Earl Grey tea... if their
refreshingly aromatic qualities are good enough for hot
brews then they're also good enough for gin.

Raspberry leaves: Slightly bitter tea-like flavours with
delicate fruity notes.

Lemongrass: Flavours and aromas of fresh lemon with
a gingery twist.

Elsewhere, tangy menthol notes can be obtained
from eucalyptus and bog myrtle; fresh woody and citrus
flavours from spruce and pine; and bitterness from
yarrow or wormwood.

Other botanicals

By now you've probably realized that when it comes to botanicals used in gin, just about anything goes. Here are a few more ingredients that may surprise you:

Almonds: Sweet and bitter almonds are among the most used botanicals for gin, providing a creamy texture as well as a mild nutty flavour.

Celery: A surprisingly useful ingredient in drinks making, celery has light and refreshing qualities that can make other flavours sing.

Frankincense: A resin from the *Boswellia* tree, frankincense is used in the perfume industry for woody and spicy aromas that gin distillers are rather fond of.

Honey: Used to infuse sweetness into finished gin, honey can also be used among the distilled botanicals, the aim being to capture the aromatic qualities from whatever flowers the bees visited to make it.

Seaweed: Coastal-based distilleries are often eager to forage local seaweed in the hope that its briny qualities give their gins an essence of the sea.

What does gin taste like?

OLD CLASSICS

To find out how those botanicals work together to create the myriad of gins available, let's start with the classic gins your great-grandparents would have drunk. These mostly taste of juniper, with other botanicals used as a supporting cast to provide depth and balance.

Take Beefeater London Dry, a gin known and loved the world over and one of the original exponents of the London Dry style. You can instantly taste the sharp fruit and resinous pine of juniper, with some additional citrus notes complementing these flavours.

Fleischmann's, Gordon's and others all provide their own variations to the upfront taste of juniper and, despite the current flavour trends that gin is going through, these staple classics still sell in vast numbers. Before you get carried away with funkier flavours, it's well worth investing in one of these to get your gin bearings.

CONTEMPORARY JUNIPER-FORWARD GINS

While some contemporary gins soften the effects of juniper to allow more flavours to shine, others continue to place emphasis on this main ingredient, accentuating various aspects of its character with complementary botanicals.

The heavy use of juniper in Junipero displays its woody, piney flavours, with spices cubeb and grains of paradise bringing out some peppery heat. Meanwhile, Swedish distillery Hernö promotes other strong flavours alongside powerful juniper, including lingonberry, black pepper and meadowsweet. These pack an even greater punch in its navy-strength gin.

Hepple Gin also highlights juniper's resinous qualities with the addition of Douglas fir and it doesn't shy away from the berries' natural bitterness either, with herby notes of lovage and blackcurrant leaf bringing out this characteristic.

A lot of these gins taste great when diluted with just ice and water, as well as making various delicious cocktails. Hayman's Old Tom is a good cocktail choice, with bold juniper, zesty and spicy flavours and the additional sweetness synonymous with the Old Tom style.

There are persons who rub the body with juniper berries as a preventive of the attacks of serpents.

Pliny the Elder

FLORAL GINS

For those who like to lead with their nose, sniff out gins with a floral focus. Some balance various floral botanicals to create complex aromas – try Bloom, which includes honeysuckle and camomile, or Silent Pool, with lavender, elderflower and camomile among its ingredients. Others, such as French gin Citadelle, expertly combine floral notes with the perfumes of citrus and spice.

Dorothy Parker American Gin introduces hibiscus into its floral mix, producing a warm, heady bouquet that works in tandem with the fruity aroma of juniper, while G'Vine Floraison uses a grape spirit base and the summery, floral notes of vine flowers to produce a gin that shares some similar aromatic qualities to a fine wine.

Other floral gins like to showcase one specific scent, cranking up its levels to make it stand out more prominently, with lavender, elderflower, violet and rose among the most popular choices.

Try these floral gins in the honey and lemon combination of a Bee's Knees cocktail, an English Garden cocktail (page 112) or simply combine with lemonade or elderflower tonic and a few different aromatic garnishes.

CITRUS-FORWARD GINS

These gins place more emphasis on the citrus fruits used, generally creating zestier, vibrant-tasting gins. Sometimes gin-makers will do little more than slightly increase the presence of the main citrus botanicals, such as oranges, lemons and limes, to lift the zestiness without upsetting the balance of the other botanicals. On other occasions a particular citrus fruit will be given much more prominence, allowing its full range of flavours and aromas to develop within the spirit.

Salcombe Gin's Start Point is a good example of the former. It's a top-notch London Dry gin but you'll instantly notice the lemon, lime and red grapefruit coming into a little more focus than in other London Drys. Japanese distiller Etsu gives more prominence to the tart and tangy flavours of yuzu, increasing the effects further in its Double Yuzu release, for extra lip-smacking refreshment.

Citrus-forward gins work well in zingy cocktails, such as the lemony French 75 (page 100), and provide an abundance of freshness when served with a light tonic.

SPICY GINS

Gins rarely have the same overwhelming levels of spices as, say, a spiced rum. Instead, the spices used provide accentuated aromatics, warmer, earthier notes and an extra depth of flavour. They tend to be quite moreish, appealing to those drinkers who like to sip slowly and sagely nod about the layers of taste they're experiencing.

Audemus Pink Pepper Gin uses interesting spices to give drinkers a game of "guess the ingredient" (if you detect a Danish pastry aroma and cola flavour it could be a combination of cardamom, vanilla and tonka beans), while Kenya's Procera Red Dot includes five different peppers for a big-hitting burst of heat and flavour.

Like other spicy gins, they are bold and confident, and their flavours can linger on the palate a little longer than most. Besides steady sipping with an Indian Tonic Water, these gins are also great for adding some punch to a simple cocktail such as a classic Martini (page 102) or Martinez (page 106).

HERBAL GINS

Just as a herbal garnish can lead your senses in a new direction, so the use of herbs by distillers can also set your palette up for a journey of discovery. Depending on the herbs used, they can soothe you while you sip or pick you up and take you to a holiday in the Mediterranean, a wind-swept coastline or a relaxing bench in a country garden. Not all herbal gins appeal to everyone but find one that works for you and it will be a gin you keep returning to.

It might be a single herb that hits the spot, such as the freshly picked lemon-balm leaves in Warner's herby, zesty Lemon Balm Gin, or the medley of Mediterranean herbs and olives in the charmingly smooth Gin Mare.

These gins work well with light or herbal tonics and are a great accompaniment to food. For a cocktail, try one in a Martini (page 102), giving it a garnish that best suits its herbal character.

FRUITY GINS

Some gins that are described as being "fruity" might use one or more fruits as part of their botanical collection and allow them to nudge the overall balance of flavours in a fruity direction. Others go much heavier on the one or two ingredients to produce flavoured gins.

In the former category is Venezuela's Canaïma Gin, with prominent juniper and a swirl of botanical fruit flavours from less familiar fruits of the Amazon rainforest including copoazú, seje, túpiro, açaí and merey.

Whitley Neill is a distillery known for gins that have more dominant flavours of individual fruits, with pineapple, raspberry, peach, mango, gooseberry and quince just some of those that feature in their extensive range. These gins work well served long with a soft drink such as lemonade or soda, as well as fruit-flavoured tonics. They can also be used to create fun twists on cocktails, such as the Tom Collins (see page 114).

DID YOU KNOW?

Ada Coleman was a celebrated head bartender at the legendary American Bar of the Savoy Hotel from 1903 to 1925, one of only two women to hold the post. Her clients included Charlie Chaplin, Marlene Dietrich and Mark Twain. Among numerous cocktails she created was the Hanky Panky, a mix of gin, vermouth and Fernet-Branca, which is still hugely popular today.

Unusual gins

Have you had enough flavour yet? Would you like more? How about gins featuring Brussels sprouts, fungi or even ants? Or, for something completely different, you could try South Africa's Indlovu Original, which includes... wait for it... elephant dung! For unusual gins that are a bit less bonkers, check out these three instead:

Scapegrace Black: This New Zealand gin includes aronia berry, butterfly pea and pineapple, distilled and blended to produce a naturally black liquid. Mix it with tonic and it turns red or purple. Its flavour is a mix of tropical fruits and spices.

Audemus Umami: It sounds like it shouldn't work. Capers and Parmesan cheese are among the ingredients in this gin, which is rested for a few months in cognac casks and is said to have a distinctly savoury taste.

Eden Mill Chocolate & Chilli Gin: If chocolate seems an unusual choice for gin then Eden Mill has gone one step further by combining it with chilli, creating a sweet sip with a bit of a kick.

Types of tonic

Ordering a G&T used to be easy – pick your gin and take whatever tonic you were given (which was probably Schweppes). But just as the number of gins has rocketed, so has the number of tonics:

Indian Tonic Water (or "classic" tonic): The original and still the most popular, with a strong, bitter quinine flavour and some sweetness.

Light or Dry Tonic: These tonics contain less sugar, making them a bit healthier. As sweetness can mask flavour, they're also good for gins with subtle botanicals.

Mediterranean Tonic: An invention by Fever-Tree, Mediterranean Tonic has proved to be a big hit with consumers. Infused with Mediterranean botanicals, it pares back the quinine, making it an ideal choice for less juniper-reliant contemporary gins.

Flavoured Tonics: Tonics are increasingly being made with specific flavours at the fore, giving G&T drinkers more room to experiment by combining key flavours from both drinks.

The perfect G&T

How do you make the perfect G&T? The first thing to consider is what tonic to pair with your chosen gin. If you've got gin with plenty of juniper then it can cope with the more intensely bitter flavours of a classic Indian Tonic; for gins that emphasize lighter botanicals, consider a lighter tonic. If you're having fun with flavoured gins then you can explore the world of flavoured tonics too – perhaps double up on the main ingredient by, for example, mixing a citrus-forward gin with a citrusy tonic. Or, go for a contrasting flavoured tonic instead, such as elderflower to complement a strawberry gin.

When it comes to how much tonic, general consensus is one part gin to three parts tonic, but it's more important to find your own preferences. Pour the gin first and add tonic until it hits the spot – it should help to accent the gin's flavours without obliterating them.

And you should also consider the right glass, garnish and ice...

Choosing your glassware

It's worth considering what glass is best suited to your next gin-based drink before you pour. Despite what some bar staff might tell you, there are no hard rules that must be obeyed, but it is true that different glasses can alter your drinking experience.

Glasses with round curves, tapering at the rim, are good for developing and holding aroma, while a large capacity allows for plenty of gin, tonic, ice and garnishes, while still leaving room to stick your nose in. Just remember to hold the glass by the stem so your hands don't warm the gin.

If the fizz of a G&T is more important to you, then go for a tall, narrow glass as it does a better job of retaining bubbles. For other cocktails, there are more factors that come into play, including appearance and tradition, and you'll find some specific glassware recommendations in the cocktail section, starting on page 98. But whatever gin you pour, the most important consideration is to choose something that you feel comfortable drinking from.

Garnishes

Garnishing your gin isn't just about making it look more appealing (although that obviously helps). The garnish's aroma acts like a primer for your tastebuds and will add more interest to your drink's overall profile.

Choosing an appropriate garnish can make all the difference, whether you use it as a taste of what's to come (a slice of lemon with a citrus-forward gin) or conjure up a contrast that will add to the gin's complexity (such as a floral flourish to a fruity gin).

Lemon, lime and mint are excellent garnish staples due to their fresh, invigorating aromas but experimenting with other options can be fun. Try other fruits such as strawberries, cherries or even slices of mango for a sweet surprise. Popular florals include lavender, camomile and rose petals. Rosemary is a herb that loves gin, while basil and lemon verbena are also hugely versatile, or go with a spice for some warmth and depth – star anise or cinnamon sticks smell as good as they look.

Don't forget the ice

There's a crucial element to making a good G&T or other cocktails that is often taken for granted: ice. But get the ice right and you can make every sip even more pleasurable.

The main job of ice is to chill your drink. Gin tastes so much better when served cold, so make sure you add enough to do the job sufficiently – filling the glass with ice is far better than floating a solitary cube on top.

It's also worth remembering that ice has a habit of melting and will thus dilute the drink. While a bit of watering down can help accentuate aromas and calm down the alcohol, too much can spoil a well-crafted gin. More ice keeps things colder for longer, thwarting dilution, while a few large cubes melt more slowly than lots of small ones. Finally, make sure your ice is as fresh as possible – old cubes from the freezer can take on unwanted flavours that taint your drink.

How to taste gin

When it comes to drinking gin, you could simply open your mouth and pour the good stuff in. But seeing as so much craft has gone into making it, it may be worth the extra effort to savour those special aromas and flavours in full.

To fully appreciate your gin, pour a measure without mixers, dilute with water (up to 50/50) and add ice. Its aromas and flavours will be at their most intense, without other mixers getting in their way.

Take time to immerse yourself in those glorious perfumes. When we taste things, much of the flavour we experience comes from our sense of smell, so breathe it in as you sip. Roll the gin around your mouth to coat all parts of your tongue. This will allow the gin to set off all your tastebuds and build a complete picture of its flavour. Repeat and you might start to detect more delicate flavours emerging, or perhaps the deeper spices building at the finish. Allowing yourself to truly taste the gin helps you to fully appreciate its flavour and be better placed to decide how best to serve it...

Personally, I believe a rocking hammock, a good cigar, and a tall gin-and-tonic is the way to save the planet.

P. J. O'Rourke

COCKTAIL
HOUR

Do you enjoy a well-made cocktail? Are you ready to mix, shake and stir up something special? If so, you'll find the classic cocktail recipes in this section the perfect place to start. They have been chosen for their enduring appeal, their ease to make, their reliance on a minimal amount of ingredients and, of course, having gin in the starring role.

With each recipe you'll find gin recommendations that will best suit the cocktail in style, along with some suggestions for garnishes and glassware. Some of these cocktails also have a few simple variations that will further increase your cocktail repertoire.

Now that you know all about the various styles of gins and how their flavours work, you can have even more fun by using these recipes as a template to invent your own cocktails. Let's get shaking!

French 75

The sharp shock of lemon, the fizz of Champagne and the heady dose of alcohol gives this popular cocktail a kick – much like the French 75-mm field gun after which it is named.

INGREDIENTS

50 ml gin
20 ml freshly squeezed lemon juice
15 ml sugar syrup
Approx. 75 ml Champagne (or another sparkling wine)
Ice

GARNISH

Lemon peel

GLASS

Flute

METHOD

1. Put the gin, lemon juice and sugar syrup in a cocktail shaker, fill it with ice and shake.

2. Strain the liquid into a chilled flute glass.

3. Top up with Champagne or another sparkling wine and gently stir.

4. Garnish with a twist of lemon peel.

Which gin?

The lemon and wine combination makes the French 75 a refreshingly sharp cocktail, which perfectly suits a citrus-forward gin. Try Malfy Gin con Limone or Bombay Sapphire Premier Cru.

Dry Martini

This may be one of the simplest cocktails around, but everyone has a theory on how to make it best. Use this recipe as a template then tweak until it hits the spot.

INGREDIENTS

60 ml gin
15 ml dry vermouth
Ice

GARNISH

A strip of lemon peel or an olive

GLASS

Martini

METHOD

1. Martinis are at their best ice cold so, in advance of stirring, put the gin, dry vermouth and a Martini glass in the fridge.

2. Fill a mixing jug or cocktail shaker with ice cubes then add the chilled gin and vermouth.

3. Stir for around half a minute until it's cold and diluted enough to your liking, then strain into the chilled Martini glass.

4. Top with an olive, neatly skewered on a cocktail stick, or a thin strip of lemon peel.

Which gin?

Most traditional gins love a Martini, while herbal and spicy numbers also work well. Try an old-school gin such as Beefeater, or a modern classic such as Junipero, before experimenting with other favourite gins.

MARTINI VARIATIONS

With the Martini being such a simple serve, it's easy to adjust to your own preferences by altering the ratio of gin to vermouth, adding a dash of orange bitters, trying out different garnishes or even shaking instead of stirring. Below are a few standard variations that you might find tempting:

Wet Martini: Use two parts gin and one part dry vermouth.

The Fifty-Fifty: Equal amounts of gin and dry vermouth.

Perfect Martini: Two parts gin, one part dry vermouth, one part sweet vermouth.

Sweet Martini: Substitute the dry vermouth for a sweet red vermouth and garnish with a maraschino cherry.

Dirty Martini: Add around 5 ml of olive brine from the olive jar to the mix.

The Gibson: Swap the olive or lemon garnish for a pickled cocktail onion or two.

Smoky or Burnt Martini: Swap the vermouth for Scotch whisky, preferably one that has a hint of peaty smoke to it.

DID YOU KNOW?

When James Bond asks for a Martini "shaken,
not stirred", it's a Vesper Martini he's ordering –
a drink invented by James Bond author Ian
Fleming for the 1953 novel *Casino Royale*.
To make it, use 60 ml gin, 20 ml vodka and
10 ml aromatized wine, such as Lillet Blanc,
or dry vermouth. Add to a shaker with ice,
shake before straining and serving, and garnish
with a strip of lemon peel. Fleming's original
instructions called for Gordon's gin, although
its recipe and strength have since changed.

Genever Martinez

Rich and sophisticated, the Martinez evolved from the whisky-based Manhattan and was the forerunner to the Martini. It's the perfect showcase for the grainier flavours of a good genever.

INGREDIENTS

50 ml old genever
25 ml sweet vermouth
15 ml maraschino liqueur
2 dashes Angostura bitters
Ice

GARNISH

A maraschino cherry or a strip of orange zest

GLASS

Coupe

METHOD

1. Add all the ingredients to a mixing jug or cocktail shaker with a couple of ice cubes.

2. Stir and strain into a chilled coupe glass.

3. Garnish with a maraschino cherry or a strip of orange zest, or, if you're feeling frisky, both.

Which genever?

This is the kind of after-dinner sipping cocktail that suits a good-quality old genever such as Bols Zeer Oude Genever. Alternatively, try a gin with a prominent juniper flavour, such as Death's Door.

Negroni

This cocktail is seriously sophisticated and not one for the faint-hearted. It's a bright red, boozy, bitter drink made with just three ingredients and minimal effort. No wonder it's so popular.

INGREDIENTS

30 ml gin
30 ml sweet red vermouth
30 ml Campari (or another red bitter liqueur)
Ice

GARNISH

A slice of orange or a strip of orange peel

GLASS

Old Fashioned

METHOD

1. Pop a handful of ice cubes into a (preferably chilled) glass.

2. Pour over the gin, sweet vermouth and Campari.

3. Stir and garnish with a sliver of orange peel or a slice of orange.

Tip: Give the orange peel a twist over the glass, with the outer peel facing towards the drink – this will release some of its aromatic oils and enhance the cocktail's aroma.

Which gin?

Play to this cocktail's bitter strengths with the most juniper-laden London Dry you can find, such as Retribution Gin, or emphasize the citrus with the sweet and sour orange flavours of Tanqueray's Flor De Sevilla.

NEGRONI VARIATIONS

Once you've mastered the classic Negroni (it should only take one attempt), get creative and stir up some variations. Here are a few to get you started:

Genever Negroni: Simply switch the gin for your favourite genever.

Sloe Negroni: Sloe gin works exceptionally well in a Negroni so try using it instead of the gin. If the result is a little too sweet, replace just half the gin with sloe gin, or try using a dry vermouth instead of the sweet.

Long Negroni: Eke out the flavour for longer by mixing your negroni in a tall glass and topping up with tonic or sparkling water.

The Gloria: This variation has a few more twists, so pay attention. Swap the sweet vermouth for dry vermouth and halve its quantity. Halve the quantity of Campari. Add Cointreau, or another orange liqueur (the same amount as the vermouth and Campari). Garnish with a twist of lemon.

The proper union
of gin and vermouth
is a great and sudden
glory; it is one of the
happiest marriages
on earth and one of
the shortest lived.

Bernard DeVoto

English Garden

This super summer sipper is well suited for a lazy Sunday afternoon or an evening get-together with friends. This is a simple version – there are countless others that can get rather complex.

INGREDIENTS

50 ml gin
25 ml elderflower liqueur
60 ml apple juice
10 ml lime juice
Ice

GARNISH

Take your pick from a combination of lemon, lime, cucumber or mint

GLASS

Highball

METHOD

1. Put all the ingredients into a cocktail shaker and give it a good shake to chill the drink.

2. Strain into a glass and top with your choice of garnish.

Tips: Make sure you use a good-quality apple juice – the cloudy, not-from-concentrate kind.

You can substitute the elderflower liqueur for elderflower cordial.

For parties, make a large batch in a jug, stirring with ice instead of shaking.

Which gin?

This is a good cocktail for those who like floral or herbal gins and is well suited to the cool cucumber notes of Hendrick's.

Tom Collins

A Tom Collins is a simple sour cocktail that is deliciously refreshing in its own right, but also acts as the perfect template for all manner of creative variations, some of which we highlight on page 116.

INGREDIENTS

60 ml gin
25 ml lemon juice
25 ml sugar syrup
Soda water/club soda
Ice

GARNISH

A lemon wheel and maraschino cherry

GLASS

Collins

METHOD

1. Put the gin, lemon juice and sugar syrup into a cocktail shaker with ice and give it a good shake.

2. Fill a Collins glass (or an alternative tall, slender glass) with ice. Strain the shaken ingredients into the glass.

3. Top up with as much soda water as you wish and garnish with a lemon wheel and maraschino cherry, artfully skewered together on a cocktail stick.

Which gin?

The original Tom Collins was made with Old Tom gin. Hayman's, Sacred, Jensen's and Cotswolds Distillery are just four that would be suitably up to the task.

COLLINS VARIATIONS

Lots of fun can be had by swapping ingredients from the original Tom Collins recipe, with flavoured gins a common source of experimentation. Take inspiration from these:

Elderflower Collins: Use an elderflower gin and swap the sugar syrup for elderflower cordial.

Honey Collins: Try using honey instead of sugar syrup, with a honey gin to heighten its effect. (You could also try a similar trick with maple syrup.)

Raspberry Collins: Squash a small handful of raspberries in the cocktail shaker before adding the other ingredients and, for extra raspberry flavour, use a raspberry gin. Swap the cherry garnish for a fresh raspberry.

South Side Fizz: Swap the lemon juice for lime juice (or use both lemon and lime juice) and garnish with mint and cucumber. With the soda it's a South Side Fizz, without soda it's simply a South Side.

Lazy Collins: Forget the lemon juice, sugar syrup and soda, and use lemonade instead.

DID YOU KNOW?

In 1862, the celebrated American bartender Jerry Thomas published the book *How to Mix Drinks or The Bon-Vivant's Companion*, generally considered to be the original cocktail book. In those days, a "cocktail" was just one of many categories of mixed drinks, along with "smashes", "cobblers", "mulls", "flips", "sangarees", and more. Among the 300 recipes within the book are gin punches, Gin Fizz and a rather potent-looking recipe for a drink simply named "Gin Cocktail". Its ingredients include absinthe, Orinoco bitters, gum syrup and one wine glass of Holland Gin.

Clover Club

Named after a club in Philadelphia, the original Clover Club is over a century old. The egg white, when shaken, gives it a foamy head on top of the raspberry-pink liquid, making it one of the best-looking cocktails around.

INGREDIENTS

50 ml gin
15 ml dry vermouth
15 ml lemon juice
15 ml raspberry syrup
1 egg white
Ice

GARNISH

Fresh raspberries

GLASS

Cocktail or Martini

METHOD

1. Put the gin, vermouth, lemon juice, raspberry syrup and egg white in a cocktail shaker and shake hard for a minute. This helps to form a foamy head.

2. Add the ice and shake some more to thoroughly chill the drink.

3. Strain into a cocktail glass and serve with fresh raspberries as a garnish – three on a cocktail stick is the classic look.

Tip: If you don't have any raspberry syrup, try using a teaspoon or two of raspberry jam instead.

Which gin?

The Clover Club suits a good dry gin and, seeing as it comes from Philadelphia, the city's Bluecoat American Dry would be a worthy choice.

Gimlet

This classic cocktail is simply a combination of gin and lime, with the original recipe stating a 50/50 split between gin and Rose's lime cordial. These days, folk tend to go for a less sweet version and introduce fresh lime juice, as in this recipe:

INGREDIENTS

50 ml gin
25 ml lime cordial
10 ml fresh lime juice
Ice

GARNISH

A slice or wheel of lime

GLASS

Coupe

METHOD

1. Put all the ingredients into a cocktail shaker with a handful of ice. Shake until you can feel an icy chill on the outside of the shaker.

2. Strain into a coupe glass and garnish with a wedge, slice or wheel of lime.

Tip: Try playing around with the sweet/sour combination by ditching the cordial and increasing the lime juice, using sugar syrup to sweeten it instead. Or experiment further by introducing lemon juice to the mix.

Which gin?

This cocktail suits most kinds of gin, from navy strength for a bit of a bite, to herbier concoctions such as Cooper King Herb Gin, in which its flavours of lemongrass and basil shine.

GIMLET VARIATIONS

Gin goes so well with lime that you can customize your Gimlet in whatever way takes your fancy while running a very low risk of going wrong. Here are a few ideas for various types of gin featured in this book:

Citrus gins: Use a citrus-flavoured gin to introduce another flavour, matching its hero ingredient with the garnish (for example, try an orange gin and garnish with a slice of orange).

Herbal gins: If you've opted for a herbal gin then increase the effect by putting a few herb leaves into the shaker – basil and mint being great choices. Don't forget to save a leaf for the garnish.

Floral gins: Using elderflower cordial in place of the lime cordial will give a lift to any floral gins waiting in the queue for cocktails.

Spicy gins: Lime likes heat so spice up your Gimlet by crushing a few peppercorns, or even a chilli, and adding them to the shaker with your favourite spicy gin.

One Martini is all right. Two are too many, and three are not enough.

James Thurber

How will you drink yours?

Do you have a new favourite? Perhaps something citrusy, served with a splash of tonic and a slice of lemon? Or maybe a punchy navy-strength gin, with loads of tonic water and a garnish of fresh rosemary plucked from the garden? Maybe you've rejected the tonic in favour of vermouth and have chosen a dry Martini? Or perhaps you've been creative in the kitchen and mixed a cocktail of your own invention?

And where did your gin come from? London? Edinburgh? New York, San Francisco or Sydney? Was it delicately crafted in Japan? Something outrageously experimental from Scandinavia? Is it made with just a few familiar botanicals alongside the juniper, or does it contain ingredients only found in Africa or the Amazon?

All this choice may just be the reason behind gin's current success. Not only is it an incredibly delicious drink, but exploring its world of flavour possibilities can, for many people, become a lifelong passion.

Hopefully this book has helped to feed your passion for gin, and armed you with a deeper knowledge to make your next drink even more rewarding – no matter which gin you choose and however you serve it. Cheers!

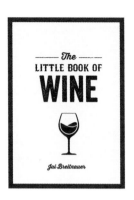

The Little Book of Wine

Jai Breitnauer

Paperback 978-1-80007-998-4

Packed with a vintage blend of culture, history and trivia, this small but full-bodied miscellany is the perfect gift for any wine fan, from the seasoned expert to the casual drinker. Whether you favour red or white, dry or sweet, sparkling or still, indulge your inner sommelier and celebrate the gift of the grape with this little book.

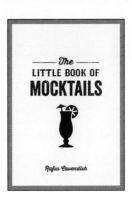

The Little Book of Mocktails

Rufus Cavendish

Paperback 978-1-80007-150-6

Master the art of the mocktail with this classy concoction of recipes and tips for deliciously booze-free beverages. Whether you're ditching alcohol completely or just looking for healthier alternatives, let these teetotal tipples dazzle and delight your taste buds!

Have you enjoyed this book?
If so, find us on Facebook at
SUMMERSDALE PUBLISHERS, on Twitter/X at
@SUMMERSDALE and on Instagram and TikTok
at **@SUMMERSDALEBOOKS** and get in touch.
We'd love to hear from you!

WWW.SUMMERSDALE.COM